BUSINESS STARTUP

The Entrepreneur's Guide to Massive
Success FAST!

Adrian J. Williams

Adrian J. Williams

Disclaimer: All attempts have been made by the author to provide factual and accurate content. The content of this book has been derived from various sources. No responsibility will be taken by the author or publisher for any damages caused by misuse of the content described in this book. Please consult an expert before attempting anything described in this book. This book contains various unauthorized biographies which are a collection of facts, thoughts, and opinions based on the lesson's learned from the noted subjects only. The written content of this book is unique to the author as it is simply a collection of facts, thoughts, and opinions. This book in no way claims to have been written, endorsed, or authorized by the noted subjects included this book.

TABLE OF CONTENTS

INTRODUCTION

Thank you for buying the book, *Business Startup: The Entrepreneur's Guide to Massive Success FAST!*

Some people may seem to have it easy. But, the truth is that everyone pays their own dues. Many people aspire to become successful entrepreneurs and only a few make it happen. This tells us just how tough it is. This can also tell you why it is very important to love what you do, do it, and actually succeed at it.

Enthusiasm is an important ingredient. But, it takes more than enthusiasm to succeed in business. There are plenty of great ideas to go around. When people stumble upon one, they have a tendency to become excited. But, this excitement does not usually last long, especially when they start to realize the amount of time, effort and money they have to invest to see the idea through.

Entrepreneurship requires creativity. It calls for courage and commitment. It demands clear and practical thinking.

This book aims to help you understand what every business startup needs, which includes strong leadership. The suggestions presented in this book are meant to help you address the most important aspects of starting a business, including testing the idea's viability as a business opportunity, writing a business plan, deciding on the business structure, naming the business, seeking funding and the like.

If you are ready to take your business idea to the next level, it is time to read on and take what this book has to offer.

Thanks again, I hope you enjoy it!

Follow me @Adrian_J_W for *free* promo updates!

CHAPTER 1
Are You Made For Entrepreneurship?

Everybody can dream of becoming their own boss. But, not everyone is cut out for entrepreneurship.

Starting a business can be both exciting and rewarding, but it can also become overwhelming and disappointing. Having your own business definitely has its own perks. You get to set your own schedule, call your own shots and so something you genuinely enjoy. But it takes more than the willingness to try to become a successful entrepreneur. Entrepreneurship requires thorough planning. It calls for creativity and a lot of hard work.

An entrepreneur must have many qualities. Listed below are some of the traits you should have if you want to be successful at owning your own business.

Independent

As an entrepreneur, you should expect to be making a lot of decisions and most of these decisions have to be made on your own. You do not have a boss. You call the shots. While that sounds appealing, it can be incredibly tough, too.

If you trust your instincts, then you may just have it in you. And, if the fear of rejection does not hold you back, then you may have what it takes to become your own boss.

Dependable

Being an entrepreneur is not just about being independent. It also means being dependable. Know that as a boss, other people are relying on you. You also need to keep this in mind when making decisions. You not only have yourself to think about. You also have to take into account the best interest of your employees. When you are the boss, everyone around you should be able to depend on you. They become your responsibility.

Risk Taker

Tough decisions have to be made every day. That means you have to deal with uncertainty. Nothing is guaranteed in business. Every decision is coupled with risks of varying degrees. Do you have the guts to make decisions even when the results are not guaranteed? Do you know what the difference is between senseless risks and calculated risks? If you are comfortable and confident with taking risks, then you may just have the spirit for entrepreneurship.

Creative

Being an entrepreneur also requires a certain level of creativity. That is, you should be able to come up with fresh and useful ideas. You will need creativity to find solutions and work around problems. You must have insights, not only in finding solutions, but also in turning issues to new opportunities.

Persuasive

A business starts with a big idea. But, it does not really matter if you have a great idea if you are unable to get people on your side. To become successful in entrepreneurship, you must be able to persuade customers and employees. You must be able to convince partners and potential lenders to make the investment. You have to make them believe in your idea as much as you do so you can get the necessary support for the business to take off. Otherwise, the opportunity ceases for your great idea.

To become a successful entrepreneur, you should have the skill to engage people. You need to make compelling arguments that are based on facts. More importantly, you should be confident about the idea you are trying to sell.

Ability to Negotiate

Entrepreneurship is about negotiation. If you are a great negotiator, you have a better chance of succeeding. When you own your business, there are a lot of things to negotiate, including lease agreements, contract terms and the rates. With outstanding negotiation skills, you are bound to save more money and keep the business running smoothly.

Build a Strong Support System

Being independent does not mean you have to be alone and do all the work. As an entrepreneur, you need to build a strong support system. You need to have the skill necessary to choose the right people to establish your support network and that includes choosing the right employees, as well as trusting the right mentor for sound advice and proper guidance.

With the above traits in mind, are you confident you have what it takes to become an entrepreneur? You should answer a few important questions before starting your business. Your answers can help either further strengthen your resolve or shed light on the things you need to focus and improve on.

Why do I want to start a business?

What exactly is it that drives your desire to own a business? You need to know your reasons. These reasons will help remind you later on, especially during the tough times, why you should keep on moving forward.

What type of business do I want?

You also need to define the kind of business you want to set up. Your desire to be your own boss is not enough. You need a big idea to define your business. And, that idea must be viable.

Who is my target customer?

There are plenty of good ideas around. But, not all of them become successful. One of the things you have to be sure of is the readiness of the market for your product or service. That means you must study and define your ideal customer clearly.

What kind of products or services will I provide?

Great ideas have practical application. They are transformed into tangible products and services that customers recognize.

Do I have the time and money to start a business?

You do not necessarily have to invest a lot of money, but you need a sufficient amount to get set up. Always start small, but have the vision to grow big.

Entrepreneurship is a full-time job. You must be willing to spend a lot of time and energy on your business. You must have the discipline as well as the resources to turn your idea or dream into reality.

What is my unique selling proposition?

Your product or service does not necessarily have to be one of a kind. But there should be a point of difference that can set it apart from other existing products or services in the market. You have to be able to find and define that differentiating factor that will make your products and services recognizable and appealing to your target customers.

Where should I set up my business?

It is also important to find the most strategic location to set up your business. Do not just go for the most affordable site. Choose where you are most accessible to your market.

How many employees will I need?

As mentioned previously, you do not have to be alone doing all the work. You will need competent people to help you get started. You have to ask yourself how many employees you need to help you launch the business.

Other important questions to ask yourself before starting include the following:

What kind of suppliers will I need? How much money do I need? Do I need to obtain a loan?

How soon can I make my products and services available to the market? How long will it take before I make any profit?

Who are my competitors? How will I price my products or services? How will it compare to my competitors?

What legal structure of business should I follow? What are my business tax obligations? What types of insurance will my business require?

How exactly will I manage or run my business? How do I go about advertising my business?

The above listed questions are supposed to help you define the details of your business. They are supposed to provide you with a much clearer perspective on the matters that require your attention. Answers to these questions can serve as your guide and reference for defining your business, the kind of business you have dreamt about.

Now that you have answered the above questions, the next step is to start determining the things you will need to make your dreams come true. You cannot start a business empty handed. You may try, but that will only lead you doomed to failure.

With this said, you need to understand the importance of a big idea and how to nurture it. You also need to learn how to write a winning business proposal and what needs to be included. An aspiring entrepreneur has to educate himself about all the legal and tax requirements of starting a new business. In other words, it is not only important that you focus on the business idea itself, you have to test it and view it from all possible aspects. All these will be discussed in the next chapters.

CHAPTER 2

Write a Winning Business Proposal

It takes a great deal of planning before you can successfully set up and make your business grow. Your business is an investment, not only of resources, but of your valuable time and effort. That means you have to prepare. What better way to ensure your readiness but a well-crafted business plan.

Many big companies had their beginning on paper. A business plan serves as your roadmap. It defines the direction you need to take towards success. You need a business plan to convince investors of the viability of the business so they will be willing to lend you the necessary capital. You need a business plan to guide you in the process.

Making Your Business Plan Stand Out

Getting to know your target market is one of the first and most crucial steps in creating the business plan. You must clearly identify your market and define the reasons that will convince them to buy from you instead of the competition. For this reason, the foundation of your plan must be strong and clear.

How exactly are you supposed to create a business plan that stands out? Here are a few tips.

Clearly State Your Offer

It is important that you deeply understand what it is that makes your business unique. Define the needs that your product or service can fulfill. Identify and communicate the unique offer and the benefits that give your business value and make it stand out.

For instance, if you are opening a restaurant in a town filled with others, it does not necessarily mean you are just one among many. It may appear to be the case if you define your offer in a generic manner. Although restaurants may essentially offer the same thing, food, some may offer fine dining, others fast food and still some sell the ambience, etc. In other words, even a seemingly saturated market can offer opportunity for growth as long as you know your differentiating factor and clearly communicate it.

Craft a Clear Strategy

Many people seem to think that advertising their business as a jack-of-all-trades is advantageous. On the contrary, it usually works to their disadvantage. It serves as an impediment to their growth. This is especially true for small businesses.

If you own a small business, a much better strategy will be to divide the business into manageable niches. By keeping your operations small, you have better chances of focusing on specific groups of customers. Your efforts become more targeted rather than scattered. In other words, being a master of one thing is far more beneficial than being a jack-of-all-trades.

Define Your Niche

On your own knowledge of the market itself, you may be able to identify a viable niche. However, it will still prove more beneficial for you to conduct a market survey. By studying potential customers more closely, you may be able to find untapped needs that you can take advantage of.

With adequate research, you can easily identify the areas where the competition has already established in. Through research, you can also determine areas that may be disregarded by the competition and can therefore be potential business opportunities.

A business plan contains information not only about what you are planning to do, but more importantly, how you intend to do it. There are basically three parts in a business plan that includes the following.

The Business Concept

This is the part where you describe your business structure and discuss the industry. It should contain information about your products and services. The business concept section should contain details on how you plan to achieve success for your business.

The Marketplace Section

Customers are crucial to the success of every business. This portion is dedicated to describing and analyzing your target market. That includes information on who they are and where they can be found. It should also define how they make purchasing decisions and so on. The marketplace section should also contain a description of the competition. Here is where you have to identify your unique selling proposition or how you propose to position yourself to get ahead of the competition.

The Financial Section

Putting up and running a business requires money, which is why this section should be well defined too. The financial section of the business plan includes the income and cash flow, the financial ratios and the balance sheet.

If these three major sections are to be subdivided, your business plan should contain the following seven key components: Executive Summary, Business Description, Market Strategies, Competitive Analysis, Design and Development Plan, Operations and Management Plan and Financial Factors.

CHAPTER 3
Crucial Elements in the Business Plan

After spending some time gathering information, you should be equipped enough to write a business proposal. This is one of the essential ways to convince lenders and investors of the viability of your business idea. Let's face it, no creditor or investor in his right mind would hand you the money unless he has reviewed the project.

Writing a business plan is not just about getting the funding you need to launch the business. This plan also draws the line between success and failure. It is about being fully prepared. With the right planning, you fulfill 80 percent of the work required to make your business idea a success.

Executive Summary

As the name itself suggests, it is a summary of what you want, which means it is one of the most important parts of the plan. That also means you must clearly state what you want in the executive summary.

This summary is essentially a snapshot of the plan. In addition, it must also touch on the company profile and goals. The objective in writing the executive summary is to give the reader a brief summation of the company status as well as where you intend to take it. It should clearly state why the business idea is a viable one and why it will be a success. If you need financial support, this section can also help you grab the interest of potential investors.

The following things must be included in the executive summary: The mission statement or an explanation of what the business is all about; company information including the founders, employees, business location, etc.; products or services; financial information; growth highlights; and the summary of future plans.

Since you are just starting up with the venture, you may not have much information to fill this section. In that case, you must focus on your own experience and background. Since you do not have information to sell the business in itself, you must sell yourself and the potential of your big business idea.

You must also be able to demonstrate the efforts you have exerted to perform a thorough market analysis. In other words, you must be able to convince the reader that you are confident about reaching success and that you have a concrete plan to achieve it, as well as demonstrate the clarity of your future plans.

Company Description

This section should contain a review of the various aspects of your business. It is similar to an elevator pitch in that it can get through to your readers and potential investors. It is a tool that can help them quickly understand the business goals as well as the uniqueness of the proposition.

In this section of the business plan, you must provide a full description of the nature of your business. It must also give a list of the needs that you are trying to fill. You should thoroughly explain why and how your products and services will fulfill the needs of the marketplace.

The company description must also include a list of the target markets that your business intends to serve. It is also important to get into the competitive advantages of the business, including the location, efficiency of operations, expertise of personnel and the overall ability of your business and the rest of your team to provide value to the customers.

Market Analysis

This is another crucial element that must be addressed in the business plan. Unlike gamblers, entrepreneurs are smart enough to take calculated risks. That means you should be able to arm yourself with information first before jumping in. Otherwise, it will just be another case for mindless suicide.

Market analysis will allow you to see the big picture. In this way, you can more effectively create a plan to play in the game successfully.

This section contains information about the industry and should demonstrate your level of knowledge about the market you are venturing into. Needless to say, this section must include your research findings with the following elements: thorough description of the industry, essential information about the target market, distinguishing characteristics of potential customers, and forecasted size of the primary target, expected market share gain, strategic pricing structure and gross margin targets.

It is also important to include a competitive analysis that allows you to identify competitors based on product or service as well as according to market segment. The competitive landscape must be assessed according to strengths and weaknesses, market share, barriers of entry to the market, windows of opportunity, direct and indirect competitors among other factors.

The Market Analysis section must also include regulatory restrictions and requirements. It is essential to determine compliance and how it will affect your operations.

Organization and Management

This section of the business plan is essentially about the organizational structure. This is where ownership details are laid out. You must be able to identify who does what and clearly define the roles and responsibilities of each person involved in the business.

The organizational structure will help convince potential investors that you are on top of things. With the structure clearly defined, they get assurance that the possibility of things falling through cracks is rather slim. For startup businesses, it is especially important to identify who can complement your skill set and how these selected people can contribute to the success of the business.

Service or Product Line

This section includes a complete description of the service or product you are offering. You must emphasize the benefits of the offer. It is also important to highlight the specific need the product or service can fulfill. Overall, it must be stated what value is offered to the target customers.

When writing the benefits of the offer, you must write it from the perspective of the customer. In addition to emphasizing the customer needs being fulfilled, it is also essential to specify the advantages of your product or service over what is being offered by the competition.

The service or product line section of the business plan should also state the current development stage of the service or product. The life cycle as well as other factors that may affect this cycle in the long run must be stated. Both pending and existing copyright, patent filings, trade secrets and other legal agreements must be included.

In addition, this section must also provide an outline of research and development activities. Expected results from future R&D efforts must also be stated. Overall, an analysis of R&D efforts must be made not only specific to your business but also that which applies to the industry.

Marketing and Sales

Customers are the lifeblood of every business. This section defines the marketing strategy for your business. Your objective should not only be to drive awareness and sales. It must also include sustaining customer loyalty.

There are different strategies you must include. One is a growth strategy that involves internal growth tactics or ensuring your business is ready internally for growth. Another strategy involves refining the details about distribution channels or how you intend to deliver the product from manufacturing to distribution to retailing to customers. Finally, a communication strategy is also essential as it defines the way you intend to reach the target customers.

This shall include a combination of advertising, promotions, public relations, etc.

Funding Request

This section is especially helpful when you need financial support for starting your venture. It needs to include not only the current funding requirement but also the funding requirement for the next five years.

The funding request section of the business plan must clearly state how the funds will be used and whether the funds serve as a working capital or as capital expenditures or for acquisitions or debt retirement. You must define a strategic financial plan for the future so potential investors and creditors can use the information to determine your ability to repay the loan they shall grant you.

Financial Projections

After a thorough analysis of the market and clear setting of the business objectives, you should be able to determine an efficient allocation of your resources. For a startup business, you need prospective financial data. When you come up with the projections, make sure that it matches what is stated on your funding request.

Expect potential creditors to examine the business plan for inconsistencies. Do not leave any room for doubt or second-guessing. Make sure your facts are straight.

CHAPTER 4
Pick the Right Business Structure

When starting a new business, one of the more important things you have to think about is the type of legal structure it will have. This decision has tax implications. It also determines the level of personal liability you will have. It affects your ability to seek funding and has a huge impact on the amount of yearly paperwork you are required to do.

The decision depends on what makes the most sense. It depends on your specific circumstances as a business owner. This choice is not to be taken lightly. It is important to think it through and may also require advice from business experts.

There are four basic types of business entities. Each one has its pros and cons. You have to consider every aspect but most importantly, you have to consider the following factors.

Legal Liability

You have to determine the amount or level of legal liability you are ready to face in behalf of your business. While there is a possibility of success, there are also potential losses that you may become personally liable for. That means your acquired personal assets may be at risk of being seized. If you want to avoid such a possibility, you may want avoid setting up sole proprietorship or partnership.

Tax Implications

As a business owner, it is in your best interest to minimize taxation and take every opportunity to do so. In this case, corporations provide more tax reduction options than what are available to both proprietorships and partnerships. In addition, incorporation is subject to double taxation, an issue that can be avoided by setting up an S corporation instead. This type of business entity also reduces personal tax liability specifically in the early years of the business' existence.

Formation Cost and Ongoing Administration

While setting up a corporation does provide tax benefits, it also comes with larger costs specifically in terms of conducting business. The cost of record keeping and completing all the paperwork is much higher for a corporation as compared to a sole proprietorship or partnership. That means you may save on tax but the amount of time you have to dedicate to take care of administrative requirements can also add up.

Flexibility

When choosing a business entity, it is critical that you consider individual needs. You must take into account the specific needs of the business and your personal needs as the owner. Always consider your concerns, goals and unique financial situation.

Future Needs

At this point, your biggest concern may be to get the business off the ground. But that does not mean you can ignore everything else. It is crucial that you think forward. Imagine where the business may be at or what it may look like three, five or ten years down the road.

Think about what you want to be done with the business in case of your death. Consider your future plans of selling your part of the business. Your current needs may change in the future. It is important that you anticipate such needs or at least have a ready back up plan.

The Four Most Common Types of Business Entities

As mentioned previously, choosing a business format requires thorough analysis and thought. While you may see some advantages, you also have to consider the drawbacks. You may have to make a few compromises, as you cannot get everything you want. But you have to find what fits right. Below is a list of the four most common business entity types and their corresponding pros and cons.

Sole Proprietorship

This is probably the most popular type. That is because it is easy to set up. As an owner, a sole proprietorship also gives you complete managerial control. The biggest disadvantage is that it makes you personally liable for the business' financial obligations.

In this type of business entity, there is no distinction between the owner and the business. As the owner, you are entitled to all the profits the business makes. At the same time, you are also legally responsible for the losses, debts and liabilities of the business.

A sole proprietorship is not only easy to form. It is also inexpensive to establish. The costs are minimal. The legal costs you have to answer for are essentially limited to obtaining permits and licenses. In this business structure, you make all the decisions. Moreover, tax reporting requirements are much easier as you and your business are not taxed separately.

On the other hand, the unlimited personal liability associated with this business structure is something that some entrepreneurs are not willing to risk. A sole proprietorship can also make it much more challenging to raise money. That is mainly because stocks are not available for sale, making investors unwilling to make the investment.

Partnership

As the name itself suggests, a partnership is a structure involving two or more people sharing ownership of a single business. Each of the partners makes a contribution to all aspects of the business. Contributions include skill, money, labor and property. Each partner also earns a share in the profits. It also means each partner has a shared liability for losses of the business.

In a partnership business structure, every owner takes part in the decision making process. This is what makes it a little more complex than a sole proprietorship. This is why it is recommended to craft a legal partnership agreement and discuss possible issues upfront. The agreement should contain details on how to properly handle or make business decisions in the future, the manner by which profits will be divided or how to resolve conflicts. It must also be clear how change of ownership should be handled or the proper way of dissolving the partnership.

Among the advantages of partnership is that like a sole proprietorship, it is easy and inexpensive to set up. Expenses are limited to creating the partnership agreement. Another advantage is that the financial commitment is shared. In other words, it is much easier to pool resources together to build the capital necessary for launching the business. A partnership business structure also allows the partners to complement each others' skill set.

On the downside, disagreement among partners can possibly ensue which is why having a legal partnership agreement is not required but is certainly critical. Profits are shared and so is liability.

Corporation

Owned by shareholders, a corporation is an independent and legal entity. As such, it is separate from the people who establish it. That means owners are not held personally liable for losses. On the other hand, a corporation is a complex business structure that is more costly to set up.

With a corporation, individual or personal liability is limited. It can generate capital much more easily than other business entities. Another major advantage is the corporate tax treatment.

As for the disadvantages, setting up and operating a corporation can be rather costly and time consuming. Moreover, this business entity requires additional paperwork, making record keeping a burden. There is also a possibility of double taxation since company profits are taxed and dividends earned by shareholders are subject to tax. This can be avoided by setting up an S corporation instead by passing income and losses through individual tax returns.

Limited Liability Company

This is a business entity that is gaining popularity. It combines the benefits of a partnership and a corporation much to the advantage of business owners. Owners are protected from personal liability. In addition, both losses and profits are passed through to owners without subjecting the business itself to taxation. It also requires record keeping.

On the downside, an LLC has a limited life. In most states, the business is dissolved when a member leaves. That obligates the remaining members to fulfill both the business and legal obligations in closing the business. However, a provision on the LLC can be included in an effort to prolong the life of the business in case one member leaves the LLC.

CHAPTER 5
Choose the Perfect Name for Your Business

The business name is the cornerstone of your business' identity. It has the power to shape branding or set the tone and first impression about your company. Needless to say, it is a critical factor, one that warrants your attention. The naming process is often surrounded by doubt and uncertainty. How do you exactly go about picking the right name for your new business? Here are a few suggestions:

Start by checking out the competition.

If you have no idea where to start, it may be helpful to check out the names of the competitors first. Go through the list and allow it to spark ideas. This task will also give you a hint on how to stand out from the rest of the competition.

Always consider your target market.

When coming up with a name for your business, it is important that you always have your target market in mind. You should make sure the selected name resonates with them. Use the information about your target to determine what will be relevant to them.

Make it easy to pronounce and spell.

There is no point in choosing a name that your customers will find difficult to pronounce and tough to spell out. Keep in mind that it is your job to make it easy for them to reach you. Stick to something simple. It encourages word of mouth.

Make it unique.

While it is important that you make the business name easy, it does not mean you have to sacrifice creativity. Your name should be completely unique to stand out. It has to be creative enough to be memorable. This will come in handy later,especially when providing a back story on your business. So, make sure the business name you pick out is creative enough and carries a special meaning you can build a good story around.

Make sure it conveys a clear message.

A name can have plenty of meanings. You have to be aware of all the possible connotations that may affect the perception of your business. Be clear about the message it carries. Evaluate how other people think and feel about it.

Be careful about a limiting name.

Your business name must be unique enough to convey what your business stands for. However, you also need to be careful not to make it to limiting. Consider the future growth of the business. When you have reached the stage where expansion is possible, you must ask yourself whether the name is still relevant.

Make sure the name sets the right tone for your business.

What is important to you and the business needs to be communicated in the name. What kind of impression are you hoping for? What is the personality you want to project? In other words, it is important you pick a name that reflects exactly what the business is all about and what it will become in the future.

Avoid using initials.

Business owners seem to have an affinity for acronyms. However, there is a certain risk to using initials for a company name. It rarely inspires emotional connection. There is also a possibility you may run into legal and branding issues dealing with two different names. You may also run into some trouble explaining what the acronym stands for.

Go for a descriptive name.

A qualifier will help with differentiating your

business from the rest of the competition. Do not hesitate to use a descriptive name to emphasize what your business stands for. Aside from using an adjective, it may also be a good idea to use a benefit of the product or service as basis for creating the business name.

However, be careful about using a name that is too descriptive. Otherwise, you run the risk of limiting yourself. Consider the possibility of an expansion and check the relevance of the name when such expansion occurs.

Say it aloud.

You know you have the right name when it sounds right, especially when spoken aloud. Make sure the name is something you can live with.

Test the name out.

Before you make a final decision about the business name, it is critical that you test it out. Try using Google Adwords to search for similar phrases. Make sure the name gets attention. Be certain it is unique enough to be memorable.

You have to give it time to sink in. It may take some time for the name to start feeling right and natural.

The brainstorming process may prove to be a little more challenging than you expect. Detach yourself and be objective about your evaluation during this process. It may be exciting to start envisioning how the name appears on your logo, business card, signage and other advertising and promotion materials, control yourself. Make sure the name is something you can legally claim. Once you have found the perfect one, do not forget to trademark it.

CHAPTER 6

Make Sure You Have Enough Capital

It requires a deep understanding of your business' financing needs to increase the odds of success. You must fully understand what it takes for you to set up, manage and grow the business.

Understanding Budgetary Needs

This is another crucial step in planning for the business. Not all businesses have the same requirement. Each has its own specific financial support needs. As such, you cannot expect to learn a universal method that allows you to estimate the startup costs simply because each business' needs vary.

To estimate your budgetary needs, you must start by determining how much money the business requires to operate for the first months. Differentiate the one-time costs from ongoing costs. In the process, you should decide whether these costs are necessary or optional. That being said you must be realistic about your estimation. You must only include the things that are essential to take the business off the ground.

A thorough assessment of your current financial situation is crucial. You must have this understanding before you even start seeking financial assistance. To help you get there, it may help for you to answer the following questions.

What exactly is the nature of your need for financial assistance? Do you need the assistance to launch the business or to serve as cushion against risks?

Is the need urgent? Business needs must be anticipated. You should not wait until the last minute. You must always plan ahead. This is the key to securing the financing you need to continue business operation.

How great are the risks? It is also important to identify the gravity of the risk because it affects the cost of the loan as well as the financing alternatives available to you.

How will the capital be used? Lenders will want to know your purpose or your specific intentions for using the money. This can give them the assurance of repayment or of the business' survival or growth rate.

Do you have absolute confidence on your management team? This is one of the most important things lenders will look into. They understand that effective management is the key to the success of a business. As such, it is important that you demonstrate the strength of managerial presence.

Is your financing need stated on your business plan? This is why it is very important to have a well-written business plan. It must be solid and well thought out.

Borrowing money to fund a startup business is not uncommon. But you also need to understand that obtaining a loan is not exactly easy especially for a startup. Lenders have to be convinced you are worth the risk.

When borrowing money for funding, there is a list of items you should prepare including: personal background information including address, educational background, criminal record and the like; a resume as proof of your business or management experience; a business plan with projected financial statements, balance sheet, cash flow, etc.; a personal credit report free from inaccuracies as such can hurt your chances of getting approval; income tax returns for the previous three years; a personal financial statement; bank statements; collateral and other legal documents including business registrations and licenses, commercial leases, franchise agreements and copies of contracts with third parties among others.

Policies of program and lending institutions may vary but what they'll want to know is whether or not you have the ability to repay the loan. They will ask for your reason for applying or how you intend to use the funds from the loan. Lenders will want to find out what assets you will be purchasing and from which suppliers. They are also interested with your outstanding debt from other creditors. It is also important for them to find out who makes up your management team and just how competent they are.

CHAPTER 7
Additional Tips for Ensuring Success

Feeling overwhelmed and lost in the process is a natural reaction. Even an individual who has the education and training in business will find the task of starting a business particularly daunting. Confidence requires real world experience. But that does not make a startup an impossible feat.

How to turn a good idea into a great business opportunity

A great business always begins as an excellent idea. Before you do anything else, you must truly believe in this venture. It will require a great deal of your time, your heart and soul as well as your resources. If you are enthusiastic about it and genuinely believe it can make a difference in people's lives, then you have better chances of persevering. Attitude is important because it will help get you through the many challenges that will be thrown at your path.

Enthusiasm is a wonderful feeling and it may be just what you need for a strong commitment. However, it is also important to separate these emotions from your idea. The same inner fire that pushes you to act on the idea may be blinding you from facts. To truly know whether the idea is worth pursuing, you can do the following suggestions.

Get real world feedback.

Share the idea. If you are confident about your idea then you should not have any problem sharing it with people you trust. They can offer their honest opinion about it. If you trust them enough then they may have your best interest at heart. That means they can give you well thought out and sound advice.

It is recommended that you share the idea with people around you whom you trust. It is also highly advised that you share it with potential users. This can give you an idea whether or not a wider group of individuals who fall under your target market will respond to the idea positively. Real world feedback can help you determine the feasibility of the idea transformed into a money-making business.

This means you have to face a certain level of risk. It means putting time and committing resources at a smaller scale. This is also how you create the perfect moment or the right opportunity.

Develop your samples and present them to the select group. Conduct small-scale market research. Check the response. Do not fret when you get a negative reaction. It may just mean you need to tweak the offer a little. A few changes won't hurt. In fact, it can work to your advantage, especially in the long run.

Aspiring entrepreneurs should listen to St. Francis of Assisi when he said, "Start by doing what's necessary; then do what's possible; and suddenly you are doing the impossible." This initial test of your idea is necessary to get the essential information you need. That is whether or not the idea is viable and worth investing in.

Start with your primary target.

Many small businesses try too hard to be a jack-of-all-trades and they end up being a master of none. You simply cannot try to be everything. While it is possible your idea has strong potential in more than one market, what you need to do first is to find your primary target. That is who has the greatest need of what you have to offer.

The success of a product or service depends on the customers. That said, it is crucial that you find out who your ideal customers are, whose needs and wants are fulfilled by the service or product you create. You must find an open market. You must help the market prepare and become ready to accept an alternative from what they are used to. This is something that must be done at the initial stage.

Are you ready to raise the money?

A business opportunity needs to be assessed against the expense of building it. While you may have an excellent opportunity, you should also be prepared to get out of your comfort zone and raise the money necessary to get the business off the ground.

This means you have to bring your strongest skills to the table. Keep in mind that setting up a business requires commitment. You have better chances of success if your focus on the things that you have more experience in.

Do a SWOT analysis.

When you plan to launch a business, it is in your best interest to test its longevity. Many startups tend to become merely fads. To avoid such a fate, you need to be realistic about it. A SWOT analysis can help you determine not only the potential of survival but also the potential of success in the long run.

Planning is one of the most essential tasks you have to do to ensure the success of your business. If you are not ready to leave your comfort zone and start doing what is necessary to turn your idea into a business, then you may not have what it takes to succeed. It takes a lot of guts to put yourself and your idea out there. The question is: are you ready to make the move?

There is no perfect formula to becoming a successful entrepreneur. Every story is different. The most successful ones will agree on the following pieces of advice.

Stick to what you love doing.

Passion is an essential ingredient. Passion can help ignite your success. Think about it, building a business requires a lot of time and energy so you might as well stick to what you love doing.

Get on with the business while still employed.

One of the biggest reasons a lot of people postpone their dreams of starting their own business is money. Setting up a business may mean you have to pull your resources together and live without money for a time before the business starts earning profits. It is inevitable in the business process. In which case, the sensible thing to do is start working on the business while you are still employed. Keeping your source of income proves to be beneficial while you are going through the first phase of the business process.

You don't have to do it alone.

No man is an island and that is true in the business world as well. It does not mean you have to find partners if you do not want that kind of setup. But at least have someone who can help you during the critical stages. Get a mentor or involve a family member or a friend, anyone you trust to help you brainstorm ideas. Everybody needs a support system.

Make sure you have one.

Get customers first.

You do not have to wait to get customers until your business has officially started. Any business will not survive without the support from customers. So you must work on building your network of customers as soon as possible. This is why networking is important for entrepreneurs.

Get on with the research.

You cannot succeed on the business unless you work on becoming an expert in your chosen industry first. Your chances of success depends on your ability to understand the industry and the market you are about to enter. You need straight facts as you write the business plan and make your great idea more tangible on paper. Do your research and gain the expertise required for you to do your job well.

Get help.

Being an expert does not really require you to be a master of everything. There are some things that you will have to let others do, including accounting or bookkeeping. Being an excellent entrepreneur means having the ability to find the right people to do the job. Do not even attempt to run everything yourself. Focus on what you are qualified doing and find the right people to do the rest.

Be professional.

You have to show just how serious you are about pursuing this venture. You have to wear the attitude of success. Always treat people in a courteous and professional manner. Get your business cards ready.

Pull your resources together.

It requires money to start your own business. That means you must be ready financially. Your savings may be helpful in getting some of the money you need. You can also ask for assistance from creditors and investors.

Always have a financial fallback plan. You simply cannot expect this part to be easy. In fact, it is particularly difficult for business startups to raise the money and get approved.

Start figuring out legal and tax issues.

The issue of money is not the only thing you have to worry about. It is also important that you figure out the legal and tax requirements of setting up a business. In addition, it is crucial you get it right the first time. Otherwise, you are in for a costly situation later on.

Make sure you understand your tax and legal obligations as a business owner. Comply with the requirements so your business can launch and operate smoothly.

CHAPTER 8

Mark Cuban's Success Strategies

Who Is Mark Cuban?

Mark Cuban is an American businessman, inventor and philanthropist who is best known as the owner of one of the National Basketball Association's most popular and prolific teams, the Dallas Mavericks. Known for his passion for what he does, Cuban is one of the most successful and richest men in America and in the world. He also owns Landmark Theaters, the nation's biggest chain of art house theaters and Magnolia Pictures, a film outfit that specializes in distributing independent and foreign films. Cuban is also the chairman of AXS TV, the country's first ever High Definition Satellite Television Network. He is also a big investor in the Television show Shark Tank, which aims to help budding entrepreneurs with starting their business.

Mark Cuban was born on July 31, 1958 in an affluent suburb in Pittsburgh, Pennsylvania to Jewish parents. He grew up in Mount Lebanon and attended school in that area. His father was an automobile upholsterer. Cuban's first dive into business happened when he was twelve years old. In order to buy an expensive pair of sports shoes, he sold garbage bags. From there, he went on to do several other jobs such as being a bartender, a disco dancing instructor and a party promoter. To pay for his college education, he collected and sold stamps and even made a thousand dollars by creating a chain letter.

He did not attend his senior year in high school and instead, went to the University of Pittsburgh. After a year, he transferred to Indiana University in Bloomington, Indiana and then to the Kelley School of Business, where he graduated with a degree in Business Administration in the year 1981. As for why he chose to go to the Kelley School of Business, he said that he chose it because it had the least expensive tuition among all the business schools in the Top 10 list.

He married Tiffany Stewart in September 2002 on the island of Barbados. They have two daughters: Alexis Sofia who was born on September 2005 and Alyssa, who was born in 2007. They also have a son who was born in 2010. Cuban and his family live in a lovely 24,000 Square ft. Mansion in Dallas, Texas.

The Mark Cuban Stimulus Plan

Another one of his trademarks is the Mark Cuban Stimulus Plan that was launched on February 9, 2009. The main goal of this campaign is to have an open source exchange of ideas.

The goal is for individuals to post ideas that fit certain criteria in the hopes that either Cuban will fund or invest in their ideas or that other people will adopt these ideas and turn them into something bigger to further stimulate and enhance the economy.

Instead of being a capitalist, Cuban wanted to inspire people by trying to get them to work together for the benefit of not only themselves, but for the world as well. He believed that by hearing people's different ideas and by knowing how many people want to do something, more people will be inspired to do what they can for the betterment of this world.

Starting a business, even a small one, can give people hope and make them realize that it's possible to succeed and that we can all be our own boss. By hearing what people have to say, people pay more attention and are motivated to start working and doing their best for their business. This campaign thrives on positivity and inspiration. Cuban proved how unselfish he is by wanting other people to have the kind of success that he had.

Cuban accepts any ideas that are environmental or scientific, concerning the Information Technology niche and more. He'll accept almost anything, as long as it's original and that you can work hard for it. Cuban wants to fund good ideas so that in time, the world can open its eyes to brand new businesses that aren't capitalists and will benefit everyone. Cuban wants to see people working hard and trying to achieve their dreams and to see action. He wants to see that people can still be inspired and that people can do what they can to help themselves get out of the rut that they are in.

Cuban believes that entrepreneurs will help make the economy better and that they are the answer to a brighter future. With this campaign, Cuban makes people realize that they can do things to help the country, that they can push themselves, and that they too can succeed. He has also gained the respect from not only his colleagues in the business world but also of people from all walks of life. Because he isn't selfish with what he had, he is able to inspire people to work hard, as well.

Mark's Lessons for Entrepreneurs

Mark Cuban is one of the forces that changed America for the better. Without him, our Internet experience would be harder and we would probably be confused as to what to do. Cuban is also evidence that business IS for everyone: He was not very rich, but he was still able to make a name for himself and became one of the richest men in the world.

We can learn so much from Mark Cuban. Here are some of the best lessons taken from his life that you should make note of:

"If you can dream it, then you can do it."

Cuban has many goals for himself and is able to attain those goals because he believes in himself. Believing in yourself is always one of the keys to success.

"Don't stop dreaming, even if you have already achieved some of your dreams."

Cuban has never stopped dreaming. He started a company but that wasn't the end. He owned an NBA team and still wants to own teams from other sports associations. He doesn't stop because he knows that as long as you are alive, then you can still do a lot.

"Never forget your colleagues."

Cuban knows how to ask for help from some of his friends and former classmates. Sometimes, two heads are better than one.

"Invest in good companies."

This is a no-brainer. If you want to succeed, then you have to make sure that the companies you invest in are big in the market and people like and respect them. By doing so, you can avoid crashing in the market and you will profit from the companies eventually.

"Learn more about your craft."

Cuban knew that learning does not end in school. When you are in the real world, you have so much more to do and so much more to learn. That's what Cuban keeps doing. He studies his craft and maintains his passion for business.

"Learn from others and don't be afraid of being inspired by other people."

Cuban looked up to Ayn Rand and has a high level of respect for President Barack Obama. The point is, no matter how successful you are, remember that it's okay to look up to other people and know that you can learn a lot from them.

"Read."

Cuban is a bookworm and finds books are highly motivational and inspiring. If you need a jolt of inspiration in your life, then why not read some books and learn from what other people have written? It's okay to do this and it will help you.

"Know how to sell."

Cuban was able to build an empire and be the top player in the game because he knew how to sell his properties when he had to, so he could build new ones and invest in others. Selling is okay. You do not have to be sentimental all the time, especially if it benefits your business.

"Help others."

Cuban is not selfish with lending his time, money and advice especially to budding entrepreneurs. We all need a little help to get by so if you know that you can help others, why not do so? Keep the positivity circulating.

"Learn how to give back."

Giving back is great. Knowing you are able to help others is good for your soul. It's always good to share what you have and not be selfish. Life is too short to be selfish.

"Be patient."

There were times when Cuban lost his patience when trying to achieve something and when his temper flared. Learn from this. Know how to control your temper and your anger. Life and business can be stressful sometimes, but it would be even more stressful if you let the stress and the anger get to you. Control your anger before it controls you.

"Learn about what's new and see what you can do."

"Don't let change ride you. Ride change and you'll see that success will come to you easily."

"Work hard."

If you don't work hard, then what will you get? Luck and success won't come knocking at your door. Like Cuban, you have to work hard and show the world what you're made of. You have to learn how to do things in order for you to succeed and not let other people do it for you. If you can dream hard, then you can work hard, too.

"Know how to laugh at yourself."

If you don't laugh at yourself, then you will be in constant turmoil. Laughing can make everything better. Try it and you'll see. At the end of the day, we all make mistakes and the best we can do is get by, live with it, and do better next time.

"You can't always get what you want."

Cuban also experienced some losses in his life such as deals that didn't go through, and so much more. This did not hinder him from trying to get what's best and for still doing his best in everything he did and still does. You can't always get what you want, but that's no reason for you to stop trying. We all have our place in the world. We all have things that are meant for us.

"Be the best in your craft."

There are many businesses competitors in existence, but you know what? If you do your best and if you try to show the world that you are the best and your company and products prove that, then more people will admire you and patronize your business. Do your best.

"Last but not least, and above all, be passionate about what you do."

What's the point of doing something if you don't feel good about it? For you to be able to do something every day, you have to love what you do. Passion transforms into good things. Passion is good because it helps you push harder, work further and become the best you can be at whatever you do. If you love what you do, then it won't seem like work. If you love what you do, then people will know it. If you love what you do, then it will show and you will be successful because you know what you're doing and you love what you're doing.

To be successful in life, you have to know these things. You have to follow these things and you have to create your own niche and a name for yourself in society. By trying to do these things, you'll see that sooner or later, you can be as successful as Mark Cuban, maybe even more. So, starting today, no more excuses. Dream big, work hard, and see yourself be successful. You can do it, just trust yourself.

CHAPTER 9
Kevin O'Leary's Success Strategies

Who Is Kevin O'Leary?

On July 9, 1954, in Montreal, Quebec, Canada, Kevin O'Leary was born into a middle class family. His Irish father was a salesman and his Lebanese mother had the fortune of owning a family business which influenced Kevin's instincts early on in life. His mother taught him smart ways of doing business and finance that tremendously helped in developing his business intuition. His parents divorced when he was seven years old and his father died soon after that. His mother, Georgette, later remarried George Kanawaty, the United Nations ILO counsel executive. With the mentoring of his two parents, Kevin's career was more directed towards business.

He attended St. George School and went on to Royal Military College Saint-Jean for two years. After that, he studied at the University of Waterloo and graduated with an Honors Bachelor's degree in Environmental Studies and Anthropology. In 1980, he earned an MBA from the Richard Ivey School of Business at the University of Western Ontario.

Before making it to the world of business, Kevin started with television production by launching Special Event Television (SET) with some of his friends. Later, he was bought out of it so he started to venture on to the software industry.

He is the founder of SoftKey International, an educational software company that published personal computer software in the 1990s. It focuses on enhancing the young generation's reading and math skills. Who would think that it all just started operating in the basement of his house with a $10,000 loan from his mother? In 1999, he got a deal with Mattel Toy Company, selling The Learning Company for almost 4 billion dollars.

In 2003, Kevin tried to venture in a new direction. He served as director and co-investor at Storage Now. The company was then known as the third largest operator of climate-controlled storage facilities in Canada.

Kevin's expertise in investment and the business sector paved the way for his new career on television. In 2006, he took a spot as a co-investor and venture capitalist at the hit Canadian TV show, *Dragon's Den*.

In 2008, O'Leary founded the O'Leary Funds where he also serves as Chairman. *Get Paid While You Wait* serves as the investment company's transaction line.

In 2008, Kevin also took part in Discovery's short TV series, *Project Earth*. He traveled the world together with Engineer Jennifer Langwell and quantum physicist Basil Singer as they assisted scientists to try to find practical solutions to global warming. Simultaneously, they also put into consideration the financial and environmental impact of the potential solutions that they came up with.

In 2009, he was also taken as one of the venture capitalists in the US adaptation of Dragon's Den, *Shark Tank*.

Also, from 2009 up to the present, Kevin serves as co-host of the Canadian reality television series, *The Lang and O'Leary Exchange*. Together with Amanda Lang, they talk about the top five business stories of the day and make commentaries. They also present viewers with different ways on how to invest their money. What spices up the show are the opposing views of these two opinionated business people. O'Leary's conservative principles on business usually clash against Amanda Lang's liberal inclinations. The show also invites guests from the business sector for a roundtable discussion with Lang and O'Leary so that their opinions can also be heard. It also adds to the diversity of the show and presents viewers with more strategies and choices.

In 2011, Kevin published his first book, *"Cold Hard Truth: On Business, Money, & Life"* where he shared tips and strategies on entrepreneurship, business, money and life. He also presented in this book the valuable lessons and practical ways on making more money that anybody can relate to and put into practice in their own lives.

By the following year, he published a sequel entitled *"Cold Hard Truth on Men, Women and Money"* where he focused more on the common mistakes that people do with their money and tips and tricks on how to solve the problem. Here he targeted that his readers learn more about money management techniques that will lead them to financial freedom and give them an edge in managing where the money goes in every stage of life.

At present, Kevin O'Leary is considered one of the most successful venture capitalists and businessmen of Canada. His story is something that aspiring entrepreneurs and businessmen have to look for because like most success stories, his started with a big idea without much money to operate and no assurance of victory. But he made it and still is at it, so people better know and learn from his success story.

Kevin on Money

"It's all about the money!"

It's the kind of statement that people often hear from Kevin O'Leary. For Kevin, everything boils down to money. He thinks that money is just a way for people to achieve personal freedom. He may appear money driven but that's the exact reason why he is in business. The world of business, investment and entrepreneurship starts and ends with money. Let's take a look at what Kevin has to say about saving money and man's relationship to it.

"Money is beautiful because it's binary – you have it or you don't. And having it beats not having it."

Kevin believes that people who have debts are making themselves vulnerable. It sounds true because money is power. It enables you to do whatever it is you desire to do at your own pace. Growing old also deserves the security of money in your bank account. It's about being able to get by with assurance from yourself. It is financial independence to the fullest.

Kevin thinks that people also have to seriously consider how they plan to use credit cards before getting one. He invests in credit card companies but also refers to them as "the devils' tools." It is one root cause of overspending. He is happy, of course, for making money from these companies and that is thanks to the people who make monthly credit card payments.

In line with this, Kevin believes that people can cut down on their simple pleasure spending in order to save money. On his interview for Kobo, Kevin explained that eventually, a person's income will not hold these expenditures and will result in debt.

He says, *"Save 10% of every pay check."* That way, people have sure money wherever they go and whatever happens.

"There are only three important things in life: men, women and money."

This is one particular statement of O'Leary that I find interesting. It exudes truth as much as humor. He thinks that marriages collapse because of money, either too much or too little of it.

"Money doesn't care about you! It can be your ally or deadly foe. It's not a friend or an enemy. You make it that."

Here, Kevin clearly states his point on man's relationship with money. He believes that people are responsible for how money works for them. He thinks that people make themselves powerless if they remain ignorant on where their money goes. He even goes on to say that people, at times, mistake their use of money for happiness. A birthday present that the salary won't afford and projection of a social status that's way beyond one's credit limits are just some of these.

He even went as far as attending Debtors Anonymous to learn more about the mechanisms of those who overspend. Through this, Kevin learned that people's emotional state can affect their relationship with money. It's like that saying, *"Money can buy happiness."* In adulthood, this could lead to enormous amounts of debt and catastrophe. Right here, Kevin wants people to see that they can have an upper hand over money, that money is what you make of it and not the other way round.

From his point of view, Kevin believes that people have to get out of bank debts early on in life. Pay the debt you made for buying that car and new home and start saving and investing on securities that will pay you interest later on in life.

Kevin's Tips for Young Entrepreneurs

O'Leary shares survival tips for today's entrepreneurs. He particularly refers to the *Dragon's Den* and *Shark Tank's* contestants on how to make the sharks and the dragons take their bait.

In one of his interviews for Phoenix Focus, Kevin specified that there are three key things he watches for in every entrepreneur that goes on the show. These are: the impression that the entrepreneur's priority is for him to make money; how well they communicate their vision; and whether they have what it takes to execute the plan.

Again, it's business and Mr. O'Leary is not on the show to make friends, but rather to make money. Going to the Tank needs not only written proposals. Contestants must have a broad knowledge of what they are talking about. They must not only believe in what they present, but must also have the edge to communicate their side in a smart and persuasive manner. It's not so easy to convince the sharks and dragons after all.

"If you aren't good with numbers, bring someone who is!"

Kevin believes that every entrepreneur has to know their numbers. He also believes in partnership. It's like drawing S.M.A.R.T goals. You make it Specific, Measurable, Attainable, Realistic and Timely. The investors on the show are not new in the business so whoever goes in front of them must be well prepared in a realistic manner.

"Even the best people are easy to replace. What I like to see is a business with a product or service that's proprietary, different from competitors, and with the right cash flow model to grow really big, really fast."

Kevin also believes that entrepreneurial success, when it comes to investment, lies more on the product or service than the person pitching it. It sounds harsh but then again, it's Kevin speaking and there is truth to what he says. Many people might take this personally but Mr. O'Leary has no room for personal issues when it's business time.

"I don't think failure is necessarily a bad thing, in fact it can be motivating. I like to see that an entrepreneur has had one big failure in their past, so that they have experienced that painful sting and are driven to never, ever feel it again."

Kevin might appear tough, bold and arrogant and that's because he really is. However, the thing is he has had a lifetime of experiences to shape him and it's not all good and happy memories. He had his share of failure and therefore sees shortcomings as a good way of learning.

When it comes to his co-investors and venture capitalists on the show, Kevin is also proud to share that they all leave a legacy to the show. In particular, Kevin believes that every *dragon* who has been part of the *Dragon's Den* brought with them a new perspective to the show and that's a good thing. Like for instance, when Looneyspoons' author David Chilton went into the show, the other *dragons* started to learn more about the deals in the food industry. Even Kevin himself was persuaded, learned from David and eventually started to make his own investments in this sector. Again, there is an emphasis on partnership. No matter how brute the man appears, O'Leary gives credit to the fact that he needs people to continuously flourish in the business.

Now, let's leave this chapter on a good note by means of seeing how Kevin O'Leary views America's entrepreneurship industry today.

"America is the land of entrepreneurship... and since entrepreneurs create jobs, I expect to see more entrepreneurship whenever the economy goes through rough times. One thing I love about Shark Tank is that it's teaching that entrepreneurial spirit to a new generation of Americans—which is just what the country needs, now more than ever."

CHAPTER 10

Robert Herjavec's Success Strategies

Who Is Robert Herjavec?

Robert Herjavec is a Canadian investor and businessman, as well as a television personality. He is a first generation immigrant who arrived in Halifax, Canada at the age of eight, and became one of the most influential business leaders in North America, having built and sold businesses to accumulate a huge fortune of over $100 million. His family arrived in Canada after they immigrated from the former Yugoslavia in 1971. Herjavec attended New College at the University of Toronto, Canada and then initially began to work for IBM, where he worked in the mainframe sales department and, thus, became more knowledgeable on computers.

This prompted him to create a software company in 1990, named the BRAK Systems, which is an integrator in Internet security software. He was able to develop this, increasing its net worth until he finally sold it for $30.2 million only ten years later. With this, Herjavec started to become one of North America's most recognizable business leaders.

Robert Herjavec was born in September 14, 1963 in Zagreb, Croatia and lived under the dictatorship of the Yugoslavian government. However, life became too difficult because of extreme poverty and the disregard of human rights, especially when his father was put in a Croatian jail. Thus, at the age of eight, when his father escaped from jail,they took a boat and fled for their lives. This was how everything took place as Robert Herjavec recalled it. According to Herjavec,

"My dad escaped from jail in a communist country and grabbed my mom and me and we came to Halifax when I was eight years old. We landed with literally a solitary suitcase. My mom remembered that she knew someone in Toronto. We got there by train, and dwelled in their basement for 18 months. It all started from there." (Mielach 2012, 1)

His family took a boat and, with just $20 in their pockets, immigrated to Canada in the hope of finding a better way of living. They settled in Toronto, Canada in the neighborhood of Rexdale. Robert Herjavec still remembered how his dad would go to work every day at a Mississauga factory during those days, earning just $76 a week. There would be an uproar in the house whenever his mom would use the $500 vacuum cleaner that they bought from a traveling salesman.. However, this change in life proved to be very complex and difficult for Herjavec.

As a young boy, he had a hard time trying to adjust to the new way of life in North America, which was very different from the way of life in Croatia. However, the experience made him realize that there are differences in economic rank between people, and this division gives them the choice on which rank they would want for themselves and their family. As Robert Herjavec recalled, "It was really interesting because, where I came from, we lived on a farm and my grandmother raised me and everybody lived like us. Then, we came to North America and it was my first impression of not being well off. I realized that compared to everybody else, we were really poor." (Mielach 2012, 1)

Having realized how poor they really were, Herjavec was inclined to do everything just to get ahead, and to make use of whatever resources he had, which could alleviate their economic status and, perhaps, make way for a better way of living. He swore to himself that his family would never be abused again, and would never be taken advantage of again. Being driven to get ahead, he graduated from college at the University of Toronto and tried to find a job, hoping that life would be much better in the coming years.

Robert on Money

With a net worth amounting to $100 million, people usually ask Herjavec how to create that much money, especially when coming out of scarcity. Robert Herjavec replies by mentioning something that Kevin O'Leary had said when they were sharing a conversation. Kevin stated that he would do anything legal just to get more money in business, but Robert Herjavec answered that businesses are not built around money but around the passion of the person to create something and then share it with the world. This may seem unbelievable at first, but this was how it was for Robert Herjavec.

His personal mission was not centered on money or profits, but on creating something new out of what he loved, which in the process would bring out something new for the world. With this, it is evident that, for Herjavec, another key to owning a great business is to center the overall mission on "building" instead of money-making. As Herjavec pointed out, 'Money doesn't keep you warm at night.' For Herjavec, this habit of centering the mission on money and profits had been the cause of why North America had been experiencing financial trouble.

As Herjavec pointed out, people in the business industry nowadays do not center on building something new or on hiring people and creating more jobs in the industry. Rather, they just want to build more money and more profit, and that, according to Robert, becomes society's fundamental problem.

It is clear, of course, that during the initial years when Herjavec was prompted to start his own businesses because of unexpected circumstances and financial difficulties, he was driven to get up and do something to prevent worse events from happening. He had sworn, when he was a young boy, that his family would never be abused and taken advantage of again, and, as much as possible, never to be desperately poor again. Thus, during difficult times, such as the time when he needed money for the payment of his mortgage, he was driven to create something and take the risk that all businesspersons take.

His personality is one that is painstakingly dependable and he cannot just sit down and do nothing when his family is facing a financial downturn. As Herjavec recalled, "I need to establish businesses, it's just who I am. I need to get up and do better; the money doesn't matter or the growth rate. I just feel I have to do a little better every day, and I don't know if that's my paranoia or being an immigrant and not having anything, but I feel that's just a part of who I am." (Sullivan and Gordon 2011, 1)

This passion and dedication may have been the

reason why his company of $400,000 grew to $1 million, and then from $1 million it grew to $5 million, and so on and so forth. For this, Robert Herjavec believes that successful businesspersons and entrepreneurs are both born and made. They are born because not everyone who is passionate and painstakingly hardworking with their business turns out to be as successful as Robert Herjavec. Yet, they are also made out of the environment and circumstances that they have faced, which built their personal principles and motives, which then became the grounds for their achievement in whatever field they are in.

Even for those who are not former immigrants, they too can build a great business through their expertise, their passion, their drive, and the type of business that they have. Perhaps, there are more insights that Herjavec may want to share with the public, such as those that concern—not money or business—but life.

Robert on Business

It appears that for Herjavec, the key to a successful business isn't money or material resources, for these things are fleeting and are usually changing. Herjavec has based this on his experiences as a businessman. According to Herjavec, most people think that the key to their success is based on how to acquire more money, but he declared that the key to success actually relies on the way the business is being run. He and his teammates have started their businesses just by using credit cards and personal savings, but their businesses succeeded in spite of having just enough money.

With this, Herjavec said that the key to a great business is having the capability and the expertise of running a great business. After 30 years in the computer industry, he learned much about how the system works, which in return allowed him to get more money through profits. However, Herjavec adds something significant when he said,

"That [computer business] was my first business and I learned that it's good to be an expert at something, especially in computers, where the field changes every three years." (Sullivan and Gordon 2011, 1)

Aside from the person's expertise, Herjavec adds something about needing emotional involvement, something that the person is passionate about. This would be a good drive for the person, which would prompt him to work unresistingly. Herjavec says something very useful to other people when he stated, 'Don't get into a business you don't love, even if you barely scrape out a living doing something you love. Otherwise, you will not be passionate about it.' Also, Herjavec insisted that it is important to have milestones; otherwise, they would have to do some changing in the business.

With this, Robert believes not just in the significance of expertise and emotional involvement, but also in creating a high point or a major objective for the business. Businesses cannot just run without direction, but should follow a certain pathway towards a specific goal. What makes Herjavec different from the rest is that, in spite of loving his business, he is also ready to let go of the business, especially during times when he had to sell his businesses to other companies. Other business persons would feel emotional about letting go of something that they had worked hard on in the previous years, but Herjavec is ready to just let go and start something new.

Change for him is as constant as the number of profits and losses. However, there is something more important that Herjavec adds in relation to business. According to Herjavec, almost all of his businesses have experienced an economic downturn; thus, entrepreneurs have to choose a business that people really need in their lives. As Herjavec stated, "One may ask, 'Are you in the business of kitchen renovation or leaky roof?' The former is something you can put off – you lose your job or get laid off, you can put that off – you do not need it, although you want it. But a leaky roof is one that needs to be fixed... Get into a business that people really need." (Sullivan and Gordon 2011, 1)

With this, Herjavec adds that the type of business is essential to whether the business would profit or if it would sell out to the public. It is not just the way the businessperson thinks, and feels, but also the type of business in relation to the given environment. Something that would be essential to the public would sell out more to the public, and would then create more profits in return. Together with the expertise, the business would definitely be profitable, especially when the businessperson is passionate about what he does and he loves what he does.

As Herjavec implied, "I own my business to the fact that I really love what I do." With this, Herjavec is driven to create and run a great business; this is the reason why he entitled his book "Driven" in 2010, which eventually became a best seller for eight straight months in Canada.

CHAPTER 11

Daymond John's Success Strategies

Who Is Daymond John?

Daymond John is an American entrepreneur known for the fashion brand FUBU. Born on February 23, 1969, Daymond John is also famous for starring and investing on the ABC reality television series *Shark Tank*. He is likewise an author of two motivational books as well as a sought after motivational speaker.

John was born in Brooklyn, New York City and spent his childhood in Queens being raised by his mother and attending Bayside High School where via a co-op, he was able to juggle his studies and a full time job. This was his first foray in business where **he** honed his entrepreneurial skills. It was no wonder that he was able to start a van service after high school graduation.

Early on, John was able to make $800 in a day by selling $10 hats he sewed at home, having seen its sales potential in the market, even if they were sold at $20. After that fateful $800, Daymond and his mother mortgaged their house for a hundred thousand dollars to kickstart FUBU. After recruiting longtime friends into the brand, they began sewing the FUBU logo on t-shirts, jerseys, and sweatshirts. To subsidize the business, John took a full time job at Red Lobster and worked on FUBU after his shifts. FUBU's first taste of publicity happened when rap artist and Hollywood actor, LL Cool J, who is also an old friend of John's, wore a FUBU shirt during one of his campaigns. He also wore a FUBU hat in one of his advertising commercials for The Gap, where in his rapping; he incorporated the words "for us, by us."

In 1994, FUBU gained further popularity and exposure when it joined the trade show in Las Vegas, where they were able to generate $300,000 worth of orders. This eventually led to more deals and partnerships with J.C Penney, Macy's, Samsung Electronics, and the National Basketball Association. After the trade show in Las Vegas, FUBU emerged to become a brand worth $350 million. Today, it is worth six billion dollars.

The popularity of FUBU also played the spotlight on Daymond John in many other ways. As an entrepreneur, he has so much to say and people are very interested in listening to him. In 2009, John joined the cast of ABC's *Shark Tank,* where he and a few other businessmen listen to pitches of aspiring businessmen and eventually decide if the business pitch is worth investing in or not. He has invested hundreds of thousands of dollars on various *Shark Tank* projects. Aside from the *Shark Tank* series, John also appeared in a few other television shows as himself like *The Game* and *The Real*.

Daymond John, the consultant and motivational speaker, is just as enterprising. Because of his reputation as a staunch businessman, he has also become an effective public speaker. People come to him, seeking wisdom and advice on ways to create additional means of revenue, brand building, marketing, entrepreneurship, and negotiations, among others. His clients include Pitbull, Shopify, and the Miss Universe Organization.

John has two published books. *Display of Power* is an autobiography, which was one of the best books of 2007, according to the Library Journal. *The Brand Within* is all about loyalty between companies and customers. Not surprisingly, John's two favorite books by other others are *Rich Dad, Poor Dad* and *Think and Grow Rich*.

John is a two-time recipient of the NCCACP Entrepreneur of the Year Award. He is also a recipient of the Congressional Achievement Award for Entrepreneurship. He received the Advertising Age Marketing 1000 Award for Outstanding Ad Campaign, Brandweek Marketer of the Year, Crain's Business of New York Forty Under Forty Award, Ernst & Young's New York Entrepreneur of the Year Award, Details 50 Most Influential Men, the Brandeis University International Business School's Asper Award for Excellence in Global Entrepreneurship, and the Essence Award.

Fubu is continually endorsed by various celebrities like LL Cool J, Will Smith, Janet Jackson, Mary J. Blige, Busta Rhymes, Magic Johnson, and Lennox Lewis.

Daymond on the Value of Time and Money

"Anything I own 100% of will always come first, and will always get whatever time is needed, no question."

Daymond John has used his time and money well in business and in his life. He used money to make more money when he, along with his mother, decided to take another mortgage for their home so that they would have seed money to launch the FUBU clothing brand. Despite the risk, John never faltered in his plans and eventually turned FUBU into a fashion power brand generating annual sales over $350 million.

John also diversified, especially in terms of marketing his brand. FUBU did not just use tradition advertising but more of the non-traditional means. As the man behind FUBU, he took on television as one of the investors of the successful television show, *Shark Tank*. Although John is known for having invested in the second highest number of businesses on the show, he is likewise known for having turned down attractive and potentially successful businesses when he sees that it will only be a waste of his expertise and, more importantly, his time. His perspective on the show is derived from the many lessons he has learned in his life; lessons that these budding entrepreneurs can learn from very well.

One of the greatest lessons to be learned from Daymond John about time is that you should understand what your time is producing. Do not be misled by what his invested time has produced. An example of these was his early experiences in business, where John drove a commuter van for sixteen hours a day. At the end of the day, he came home with 300 bucks and a sore body from having driven for hours on end. After evaluating those sixteen hours, he realized that after expenses for the van, he had been working hard for only fifty dollars a day. In comparison, when he worked for Red Lobster, he only had a one hundred dollar paycheck but he knew exactly what he was paid for his time. And it was stress-free.

Another lesson from John is to make sure the sacrifices you are making are worth it. For example, when John noticed there were chunks of his time that were unproductive, like commuting amid traffic, he decided to move closer to his office and used more of commuting time productively.

The next time lesson from John is that you should be decisive about how you spend your time. Make sure it will generate something in return for you, either financially or emotionally. Make sure that time returns something you expect and want. An example of this within John's life is in his acquisition of various homes through the years of business success. The more financial success you gain, the more you want to acquire things. However, as John would realize in his acquisitions, it requires a lot of time managing these homes. Instead of enjoying these homes, a lot of time and effort drain out the enjoyment and relaxation, which, in the end, is not really worth your time after all.

When it comes to time, John is known on his television show *Shark Tank* as very decisive. He has said, *"If my time is part of the deal, I will only consider it if my specific experience and expertise will very clearly add business value."*

If he does not know anything about the business, no matter its potential, he will usually not get involved with it. He says that his commitments are directly related to the level of accountability, risk, and investment.

Daymond on Business and Life

"I did not know much about manufacturing—I did know how to sew, but that's different than manufacturing. Sewing is an ability; manufacturing is a knowledge. Manufacturing is about how much per square yard you are using and how to do technical packages. For example, you need the knowledge of how to interpret your designs for overseas, how to be cost effectively, how much embroidery machines may cost per hour to run, how much it costs to ship the product back to the States, etc. Luckily, one of my partners went to FIT and he knew that side of the business. Also, working with Samsung, they were able to pass on that knowledge to me. It worked out well having that part of the company focus on that aspect, because it allowed me to focus on our marketing initiatives and how to keep the brand fresh."

On a good business idea:

A good business idea, according to Daymond John, is something that solves a problem or makes you do something faster and more efficiently. This should also satisfy a need like producing an existing product but making it cheaper. A good business idea should make the quality of people's life better.

On the initial steps that the entrepreneur should take:

Educate themselves in the product and industry they are getting into.

On the traits of being a great entrepreneur:

Constantly educating themselves; driven; open to advice; resourceful; doing something they love

On where to get help in creating a business plan:

Get help from small business consulting firms. Make sure to hire a consultant who specializes in the business you are getting into.

On what makes investors risk their money on a business deal:

Belief and trust on the Chief executive officer, knowing he or she has the capacity to make the business grow and that you have a patent that can be licensed out to a larger company.

On how to know of the market's need for your product or service:

Try putting it on sale online and evaluate the random people who try to purchase it.

On competing with the big fish:

Don't try. Find strength in knowing you are small and in the abilities that you have and they don't.

On creating a business plan that works:

Allocate time and money as investment on the business. List strengths and weaknesses then find a partner to take care of these weaknesses.

On building a great team:

This takes trial and error. Let people know their roles and make sure the people you hire complement your weaknesses. Hire people who are focused and want to work with you for the right reasons.

On dealing with challenges:

Let passion push you through incredibly tough times. If what you are doing does not push you through the hard times, then maybe it is time to reevaluate.

On the challenging first steps:

The initial struggle is to get past the stage of imagination to the point of conception; turning an idea into a reality. This is always the toughest phase so make sure you get past this stage successfully.

On focusing on your business and giving up your day job:

Do this if the business is already making ends meet or if you feel that you need to dedicate more time to the business. Know what exactly you are getting with what you are doing and with what you doing with your time. If the day job provides you with the financial backbone when starting up your business, then do not let it go. However, if you realize that the hours you spend in the day job is not well compensated and is usurping all your energies from working on your business then it is definitely time to give it up.

On the importance of social media:

Use social media to know more about the market and how your products and services affect them. Ultimately, it is a tool that lets you know if they like your brand or not.

On how he evaluates the aspiring entrepreneurs on television:

What void in the marketplace that their product fill; core market and has this company correctly marketed their products to them; product sales; distribution channels; how much does the entrepreneur know about his own industry; current status of the business: on the upswing, peaking, etc.; room for profit and growth; plan for growth – has it been laid out or just running in the head of the entrepreneur; is the evaluation of the company fair; how can I best help the company?

On his relationship with his mother:

Even if Daymond John had partners, his original partner in life was his mother, who readily gave him seed money for business by taking on a second mortgage for her house the moment her son was in dire need.

On his relationship with LL Cool J:

You cannot put a price on friendship and loyalty but if you can it is worth millions of dollars. The fact that a budding star such as LL Cool J trusted his brand by wearing it in a GAP commercial is a risk for both the aspiring rapper and entrepreneur. It was risky and intrusive but it was a massive leap for the brand that was indeed worth it.

On establishing relationships with distributors:

John's goal was to be distributed in Macy's but initially, these big distribution channels will say your products are not for their stores. This is discouraging. When this happened to John, he directed his focus on the mom and pop shops or the small chain stores that welcome diversity and because they are small, they get to know the brand better and in effect, will be able to sell them well to the customers. In the end, there is no small or big distributor. If you find the right one for your brand and are able to establish a good relationship with them, then your brand is in good hands. Eventually, when the big department stores hear about your reputation, like Macy's did about FUBU, they will come around and receive your brand with open arms, knowing that your brand has the capacity to give them good business. Macy's eventually supported FUBU. In the end, it is always better to prove your worth by delivering results and getting not only business but also respect instead of begging for favors all the time.

On his relationship with customers:

The most important thing for John is to build comfortable working relationships. Establishing good customer relationships provides a big advantage to the business. Providing the best service to them means giving them good value for their money and making them feel that they are valued. This means that such traits as politeness and courtesy to customers are very important. It is also important to deal with their complaints and issues at once. A relationship entails trust and if a business wants to establish customer loyalty, you have to let them know you are trustworthy. Make sure that it is easy for them to give you feedback and make sure that feedback is taken care of as soon as possible. If these are not addressed right away, make sure to assure the customer that you are working on the issues. It is important to keep your promises when it comes to customer loyalty. Like any relationship, the one between business and customer is fragile but it has its rewards. Customer loyalty is convertible to cash in the long run.

CHAPTER 12

Barbara Corcoran's Success Strategies

Who Is Barbara Corcoran?

If you have not heard of Barbara Corcoran, then you haven't been paying enough attention. This woman has made herself one of the biggest names in the male-dominated real estate market. She is also famous as one of the investors on ABC's hit reality show *Shark Tank*, and on CBC's *Dragon's Den,* and is a regular consultant on NBC's *Today*.

There is a lot more to her than that, though. In addition to being the head of a 5-billion-dollar real estate business and a television personality, at 64, Barbara is also a noted investor and business consultant, a much sought-after speaker, a syndicated columnist writing for several magazines, a bestselling author, a television personality, a wife, and a mother of two. The best part of all this is that she loves every second of her busy life.

There is no doubt that you can learn so much from Barbara Corcoran's life and what she has achieved, from the time when she was waiting tables and struggling to make ends meet to her continued and growing success today. In the next chapter, we'll take a look at how she became a real estate superstar, and from there, we'll look at her formula for staying on top of her game.

Barbara Corcoran did not have an easy start in life. She grew up in Edgewater, New Jersey as the second eldest of 10 siblings living in a 2-bedroom apartment. She was dyslexic in a time when the condition often went unrecognized and undiagnosed, and the resulting straight D's she got at school led others to believe she was stupid. By the time she turned 23, she had held 20 jobs –everything from waitressing to being a housemother at the local orphanage – and a stable future with a steady monthly income to look forward to seemed very unlikely.

A Serendipitous Start in Real Estate

For many other people, it would have been easy to let this situation overwhelm them, and they would have simply kept working multiple low-paying jobs until they reached retirement age, but not Barbara! She was constantly on the lookout for ways to improve her situation, and she did not hesitate to grab opportunities with both hands.

It was pure chance that led to her involvement in real estate. While working as a receptionist for a building manager in 1973, she asked the building manager's son, who owned a brokerage firm of his own, if he would let her work for him on the weekends. He agreed (the clincher may have been that Barbara offered to work on commission), she took the necessary licensing exams, and earned over $600 dollars in commissions on her first weekend – well over what she had been paid for 3 weeks as a receptionist!

This must have been an almost magical revelation for the young Barbara. Here was a lucrative job that took her out of a boring work routine, made use of her excellent people skills, and, if she played her cards right, would let her be her own boss. That was what she wanted most of all.

The Famous $1,000 Loan

In 1978, she borrowed $1,000 from then-boyfriend Ray Simone, and used the money to start a real estate brokerage with him. They dealt in rentals until a client came to Barbara looking for property he could buy and, despite not being prepared for that kind of transaction, she helped him find what he needed. Handling properties both for sale and for rent soon helped the company expand into a successful business, and Barbara might have been content to stay there – if her boyfriend hadn't suddenly broken the news that he intended to marry their secretary.

Barbara immediately decided to end both her personal and professional relationship with the man.

There was simply no way she could trust him again! In less than 10 minutes, they split the company in half, divvying up their agents like recruits in a football draft. As a parting blow, Simone told her, "You will never succeed without me."

Barbara wasn't about to take that lying down. She took Simone's words and turned them into her motivation – after all, success is the best kind of revenge. As she said in a recent interview, "I would rather die than let him see me fail." Quickly turning the situation around, she began to shoot for large-scale success with her very own company, The Corcoran Group.

Moving On and Moving Up

It was an utterly ambitious move in a time when all the real estate firms in New York were owned by men and when women were often relegated to the role of agent in order to attract customers, but Barbara never let that daunt her. Instead of trying to quietly blend in, she made herself highly visible with short skirts and bright clothes (eventually, she would have 14 of her trademark red suits in her wardrobe). Men working in real estate might not have liked her presence, but they were certainly aware of it. There was no way they could ignore this powerhouse of a woman. In her company's first year of business, she and the 7 agents working for her made $350,000 in revenues.

That was only the beginning for Barbara Corcoran. It soon became abundantly clear that she was a force to be reckoned with. By constantly pushing boundaries, taking setbacks in stride, fearlessly pursuing innovations, hard-line business practices, and encouraging her agents to work together instead of focusing on competition, Barbara showed that she was the equal of any man in the business.

In 1993, the Corcoran Group became distinguished as the first real estate firm to sell properties online, taking to the internet 2 years before any of its competitors. By the time Barbara decided to sell for a whopping $66 million in 2001, the company had 1,000 brokers and was making $5 billion in sales.

Barbara Corcoran Today

That on its own would already be a happy ending for anyone, but, as always, Barbara was driven to do more than rest on her laurels. Far from being content to stay at home, she has since cemented her status as a business tycoon through savvy investments and productive consultancies. She also constantly seeks out opportunities to share her wealth of knowledge and experience, never hesitating to appear as a guest speaker at business gatherings, especially those targeted at entrepreneurs. Barbara was one of the most enthusiastic respondents to ABC's invitation to be on *Shark Tank*, and she regularly appears on NBC's *Today* to relate the latest trends in real estate. She is also extremely active as a writer: in addition to her 4 books, she is a regular contributor to several magazines.

Barbara on Startups

Perhaps the most notable thing about Barbara Corcoran's career is that she never wasted time waiting to make things happen. Instead of waiting for the right time or the right resources to take advantage of an opportunity, she went right ahead and created them for herself. As her mother always said, Barbara had a great imagination, and the way she applied it to her business dealings was nothing but superb. Through this intuitive and seemingly impulsive method of expanding before she was 100% ready, she created a constant source of motivation for herself and opened up a slew of opportunities for her company.

As early in her career as 1973, Barbara was taking every chance she could to grow her business. One strategy she employed was to hire a new agent every time she had $180 to spare on a three-line advertisement in the New York Times. She would then put that agent's name in the advertisement, making her new employee happy and opening the door for more earnings in the Corcoran Group. Evidently, this strategy of taking such risks has paid off!

It's true that jumping into something totally new with little to no preparation is risky, especially in a high-stakes market like real estate; but the fact is that in real life, you are very seldom 100% ready for anything. There are always things that you won't see coming, or factors that you fail to take into consideration. The lesson you can take from Barbara in this respect is to not let the fear of the unknown cripple you. Take those chances, and make those leaps of faith: they just might be the best decisions you make.

Business Plans Are Overrated

It is worth noting that Barbara Corcoran managed to get where she is today without once relying on a concrete business plan, and she still detests reading financial reports. She also did all of this without the benefit of an MBA, proving that business and financial success is in no way dependent on your academic abilities or your talent in drawing up clearly delineated plans. In her experience, it is far better to visualize what you're aiming for, and staying motivated to achieve your goals.

As the Corcoran Entrepreneur Report showed in 2012, 38% of those who started businesses didn't even graduate from high school, and a whopping 67% were immigrants. These groups of people practically run on motivation rather than economic expertise, and, in most cases, they are more motivated than their educated counterparts with resident status.

Do Your Own Public Relations

One way in which Barbara Corcoran created opportunities for her firm's expansion was through aggressive public relations campaigns. Instead of paying PR firms for creative advertising, however, she did the Corcoran Group's PR herself, talking big and sounding smart.

In 1981, she started publishing the Corcoran Report. This report covered trends and statistics in the New York real estate market, and since they came from a credible source with her ear to the ground, so to speak, they quickly started getting attention. Publications (including the New York Times) and even other companies started coming to Barbara for facts and statistics, and she always made sure that the Corcoran Group had its byline.

The biggest publicity boost from Corcoran Report arguably came when Barbara wrote the "Madonna Report". Though she had no previous experience in selling property to a celebrity, Barbara put together a well thought-out, well-researched article on what a personality such as Madonna would look for when buying a New York apartment. The television networks quickly picked up on this, and Barbara found herself being interviewed for three separate programs. This TV airtime soon had celebrity clients lining up for her services!

By doing your own PR and by making yourself a noted expert in your line of business – which can be anything from dog-walking to barbecue sauce – you will create a larger-than-life image for your company. This image ought to be what you want your business to become, and you will keep yourself on your toes working to achieve its reality. Just be sure to deliver what you promise!

Presentation Is Important

Though appearance is not supposed to matter in such aspects of life as love and friendship, there is no doubt that presentation is very important in business. This goes from everything from your brand name to the way you dress for meetings with clients: a tacky or dull brand name will not stick in customer's minds, while dressing sloppily for business transactions smacks of disrespect for the people you are dealing with, and gives the impression that you aren't serious about what you're doing.

Barbara recognized this simple fact very early in her career. One of her very first investments after getting into the real estate business was a chic Bergdorf Goodman coat with a fur collar. It was her single expensive item of clothing, and she put it on every single day she went to work. Wearing it to meet her clients, she looked the part of classy, savvy, trustworthy real estate agent long before she had actually achieved that status, and that helped her close plenty of deals.

She still holds to that principle today. For instance,

the stained apron worn by a hopeful entrepreneur on *Shark Tank* immediately put her off despite the fact that his business had potential. Barbara maintained that the sort of business owner who couldn't be bothered to at least buy a new apron before making an appearance on national television wouldn't have the energy and trustworthiness necessary for success. Think about it. You know she's right.

It's importantto pay scrupulous attention to how you present yourself and your company in your business dealings. Doing so will project an image of respectability, responsibility, and even affluence – things that you should bring to the table for any sort of transaction.

Don't Be Fake

While a lot of what we've talked about in this chapter seems to revolve around bluff and bluster, you must never mistake false representation for creating opportunities for expansion. Don't be fake! Pretending to offer something that you can't deliver, or doing something simply because your competitors are doing it is never a strategy that pays off in the long run. People have an amazing capacity for sensing what is patently untrue, even if they can't put a finger on what's bothering them.

Instead of putting up a false front in order to drum up more business, try to think about what you can offer that is fresh and unique. Play to your strengths.

Again, you will not succeed in business by pretending to be what you're not. As Barbara's mother once told her when she was still waiting tables and dismayed over losing customers to another waitress at a local diner, "If you don't have big breasts, put ribbons on your pigtails." The young Barbara took this advice to heart, and you will see it in the singular way that she handles her work. This saying is also the title of Corcoran's bestselling book on successful business techniques.

Barbara's Advice for Entrepreneurs

If you ask Barbara Corcoran, the biggest difference between the truly great entrepreneurs and the ones who just manage to squeak by is not the number of failures they can take before giving up: it's how long they take to absorb the impact of the last failed venture before moving on. The same is true of her agents. The best ones, she says, are those who can get hit and get back up quickly, without dwelling for too long on having gone down in the first place.

Looking at her life story, you will see that the ability to rebound fast is a quality that Barbara herself possesses. She did not let bad grades be the first and only measure of her abilities, and continuously aimed to achieve more than what her schoolwork predicted for her. She had been fired from more jobs when she was 23 than the vast majority of people will ever hold in their lifetime, but instead of letting that bog her down, she chose to learn from the experiences and move on. Let's not forget how she turned one of the most painful rejections of her life into the driving motivation for success.

As long as you're striving to achieve something in business or in life, you will not be able to completely avoid making mistakes. Failure will happen, and you are allowed to feel hurt and dismayed when it does – you can't help that. Do not let the rest of your life be consumed by self-pity, and do not let one failed venture put you down for good. Take the hit, and bounce back up again. Always be ready to turn your misfortune into a golden opportunity.

For a concrete example of how Barbara turned what could have been a crushing failure into wild success, let's take a look at what led her to put the Corcoran Group on the internet.

Homes on Tape to Corcoran.com.

Barbara could tell you a lot of stories about how some of her ventures made her fall flat on her face – from the frustrating, unproductive day she spent driving Janet Jackson, her bodyguards, and her boyfriend around New York in a bulletproof van to the disastrous first World Conference of International Real Estate Leaders – but her favorite tale by far is the one that explains how she became an online pioneer. In the early 1990's the Corcoran Group invested a lot of money – approximately $70,000 – in creating Homes on Tape. These were expensively produced, highly-polished videos of all the properties the Corcoran Group had on offer, complete with the floor plans and all sorts of pictures. It was supposed to make life easier for those looking for a home in New York. They wouldn't have to go all the way out to a property to view it; they just had to pick up a video tape, pop it in their VCR, and make the decision from the comfort of their own home.

The idea behind Homes on Tape may have been sound, but in practice, it was a bomb. Clients didn't want to go to a real estate firm to pick up a video, and agents were reluctant to lend out the tapes for fear that rival companies might get their hands on them. The expense and effort needed to keep the collection of videos up to date was also immense for a project that yielded very little in terms of returns.

Fortunately, Barbara kept her head, and quickly set herself to finding a way to turn the situation around. Someone had recently told her about the possibilities offered by the internet, then taking its first steps, and she leapt at the alternative. She had all the videos converted. She then uploaded the videos onto www.corcoran.com where viewers – who already had an internet connection at home or at their place of work – could filter them based on the features they wanted in their new apartment or home.

Yes, you read that right. One of the biggest innovations in the history of the American real estate market came about as a cover-up for one whopping mistake!

Why So Serious? Fun Is Good for Business!

When it comes to her business, there is no denying that Barbara Corcoran's methods can be strict and no-nonsense. Some would even go so far to say that her practices are downright harsh. For instance, she makes no secret of the fact that she culls the lowest-performing 25% of her employees every 6 months (she calls this "shooting the sick dogs early"). She is similarly hard on habitual complainers, firing them the minute she spots them, never mind how much revenue they bring in.

As policies in the workplace go, that sounds absolutely terrifying, but Barbara has a reason for this. Chronic underperformance and negativity are not good for business in ways that go beyond the simple creation of profits: they create bad conditions for work, killing optimism and discouraging belief in the future. If allowed to go unchecked, these bad attitudes start to affect others in the office as well, and the resulting atmosphere can be poisonous.

What Barbara does encourage is fun. "I've never had a good idea at my desk!" she says, maintaining that she gets better ideas pulling weeds in her garden than she does sitting in her office.

Far from chaining employees to their desks and demanding that fresh ideas be presented in claustrophobic committee meetings, Barbara makes sure that they have the time of their lives at work. She knows full well that fun and a positive atmosphere are great for business.

With that in mind, the employees at her company find themselves treated to surprise field trips, and their office parties are always riotously fun. Her workers enjoy sharing the stories about these parties, including one where they had to go in their underwear! As far as building trust and camaraderie go, these outrageous events are far more effective than many other companies' periodic team-building exercises, and Barbara knows this. As she will tell anyone who asks, her team's best ideas and breakthroughs came "when we were laughing, when we were drinking too much."

Love Your People and They Will Love You Back.

Barbara takes great pride in going above and beyond how other bosses treat their employees. The last thing she wants is to make her workers fear her. Rather, she wants to be "surrounded by people who want to give her kisses". The little extras that she offers her team – like 15-minute massages given right at their desks - all show appreciation for their work like a gentle "I love you". And it's a simple fact of life that if you love people, they will love you back. In the workplace, this will lead them to aim for better performance, and in a lot of cases, this will lead to better customer service as well. Happy people who know that their boss is pulling for them will be more willing to go the extra mile for clients, and happy clients will be more likely to come back for repeat business. It's a very simple matter of paying it forward.

Recognition Is A Great Motivator.

Everyone else offers employees commissions and

bonuses for work well done. This is a good practice – everyone can use and will appreciate a bit of extra income, especially if it is well-deserved – but very few others will take the time to laud them for their efforts in truly meaningful ways; and, before you ask, adding a name to a trite "Employee of the Month" plaque does not count as meaningful!

The right kind of recognition will make people happy to work for you, and what's more, it will motivate them to do their best for the company. Barbara put this into practice very early when she made a habit of putting individual agent's names in her company's advertisements. Such a public show of trust and appreciation definitely contributed to her agents' willingness to give the Corcoran Group all they could offer.

Minimize In-House Competition.

It is also sound practice to minimize the importance of competition in your workplace culture. Other companies in the same line of business are already eyeing you warily and sizing you up to see exactly how much of a threat you are. You don't need your team to be doing the same amongst themselves!

The wrong kind of competition can be incredibly toxic, leading to mistrust, malcontent, and efforts to putting colleagues down instead of improving performance. You don't need the members of your team to be stabbing each other in the back just for the sake of a promotion that's being dangled in front of them as an incentive! Barbara made it a point to ensure that those at the top of her company's ladder got along incredibly well with the rest of the workforce so that they had no trouble cooperating in order to get the company to where it needed to be.

Caveat! Having Fun Does Not Mean Blurring the Line Between Professional and Personal.

Before you go about doing business with a healthier, happier attitude, however, you should avoid blurring the line between the professional and personal aspects of your life. Making sure that you and your colleagues have a blast at work doesn't mean for an instant that you can let your professionalism slip, or that you can be lax in your business practices.

Having fun is great for productivity, and it's vital to take time for your interests outside work. Barbara herself makes time for her hobbies of gardening and skiing, both cross-country and downhill, but it is equally important to lay down the boundaries that separate work and play.

Barbara Corcoran says that work-life balance is not a thing that exists, and she learned this when after years of in vitro treatments, she gave birth to her son Tommy at age 46. Trying to be a mother and the No. 1 real estate broker in New York at the same time was exhausting, and, to her dismay, she realized that she was doing both jobs at much less than the full extent of her abilities. This was a major factor in her decision to sell the Corcoran Group. Today, Barbara has very clear boundaries between her work and her family: she won't check her cell phone for work calls when she's at home, and she won't take time out of a business day to take family calls either. Doing this has helped her become much more effective in both her roles in life.

Always Remember: You Have The Right To Be There.

On the way to the top, Barbara Corcoran experienced many setbacks, some worse than others. Of all of these, she will tell you that the hardest hurdle to overcome came from inside her. It was fear: fear that she wasn't good enough, fear that she didn't belong in real estate, fear that a woman with no degree and very little experience truly did not have a chance in an industry dominated by serious men with sharp suits and MBAs.

What got her through this was something her mother told her: "You have the right to be there."

From an early age, Barbara's mother taught her and her siblings that though they might be at a financial disadvantage (a family with 10 children can very seldom be wealthy), they had as much right as the next person to get what they wanted. Barbara took this piece of advice to heart, developing her own brand of arrogance that helped her play with the big boys of real estate and prove herself better than any of them; and the saying is one that she readily passes on to other entrepreneurs, especially business owners who are just starting out.

Don't Overanalyze.

One of the most dangerous things an entrepreneur can do is fuss over analysis. Taking the time to evaluate a situation before making a business decision is all very well, but once you start to over-analyze things, you will paralyze yourself and kill opportunities. What you need to do is stop agonizing over how you are going to walk through a door to an opportunity, and simply go ahead and walk through it.

Sometimes, like Barbara, you will find the courage to stop over-analyzing decisions if you are desperate enough that you are ready to try anything. When you think about it, this is why so many immigrants and people without a high school diploma are so ready to start their own businesses. As she says in many of her talks, sometimes you just have to shove logic aside, take that leap off the cliff, and trust that you'll find the solution on your way down. It may not be easy to do this, and it will definitely be scary, but it's loads better than never trying at all.

No Negative Self-Talk!

Detractors and naysayers can often get you down, but it is often the case that the hardest naysayer to ignore is yourself. You can be hyper-aware of your faults and shortcomings to the point that you talk yourself out of trying to achieve anything, much less start a business venture.

For many people, this is the most difficult hurdle to get over on their path to success. It is very easy to stay mired in a bad patch, and Barbara knows this from experience. She says that there were times when she was unsure that she could keep her company going, but she had to get up and push past the negative self-talk. You will find that you'll need to do the same thing for yourself at many instances in your career, but remember that sometimes you can be the person with the worst opinion of yourself. It might help to think that other people – up to and including your colleagues at work – actually have a much higher opinion of yourself than you do, and it is highly likely that the better version of you that they believe in is the more accurate picture.

You Have A Right To Your Success.

It is hard to get around how some people seem predisposed to success, rather as if they've received some sort of private license to be an achiever. Forget that paradigm. Nobody has a God-given right to be more successful in life than anybody else. It's true that some people can come from wealthier backgrounds, and some people can be better educated, but that doesn't mean a thing when it comes to what you can achieve. You have as much right to success as the next person, and you should never let anybody convince you otherwise.

Barbara often relates the story of how she met real estate mogul Donald Trump. He had her called to his office because the Corcoran Report had placed his properties at No. 8 or 9 in a list of the Top 10 living spaces in New York, when he had been busy boasting that he was at No.1! Barbara says that she was terrified of the meeting (and you can bet that Trump did his best to intimidate her), but on the way up in the elevator, she remembered what her mother said. She had a right to be there. She had a right to publish what she did about Trump's properties, because she was just as much of a real estate mogul as he was, and she knew what she was talking about; and because she kept telling herself that, she had the courage to stand with Donald Trump, and come to an amicable solution to the issue.

Remember, this lesson doesn't just apply to facing down multi-billionaires who have taken issue with a detail in your article. In business, networking is vital, and you should go about it like there's no tomorrow. Don't slink out of chances to make new contacts just because you feel like a conference is too intimidating to attend, or because you think that they are out of your league. Don't be afraid to enter competitions that could potentially earn you wider recognition in addition to a juicy prize. Don't think that you don't deserve success just because the world has put you in a position where you do not seem to be predisposed towards achievement.

Again, you have to believe that you have a right to be where you are. You have every right to strive for success, and you most certainly have the right to achieve it. Hold this in your heart like a mantra, and it will be hard for the world to get you down.

CHAPTER 13
Shark Tank & Dragons' Den Explained

The original version of *The Dragon's Den* show comes from Japan and ran from 2001 to 2004 where the investors were called the *Tigers*. The format of the show is owned by SONY Entertainment. With the reality TV show's great impact to its audience, it has been adapted through the years in different countries including the United States and Canada.

The program features resident venture capitalists who listen to aspiring entrepreneurs and their business ideas. These entrepreneurs' goal is to secure funding for their work. It's one of those tricky and smart reality shows that revolves around strategies and the psychology of persuasion that can actually incite business minded discussions even at home.

The first step to get onto the show is through application. Listed already are screening questions about the nature of their proposal and how much money they are asking for it. Thousands of applicants, unfortunately, don't make it on the show. On the show, the contestants need to raise the amount they named for their ideas. They also have to name the percentage of the company's stock that will go to the investors.

More about the show, contestant entrepreneurs present their business plans to these sharks and make deals on cam. Viewers get an insight on how it happens on pitch meetings between the investors and the starting entrepreneurs. If they get the raise, it's their first step in securing funding but if not, they go home empty-handed.

As the meeting progresses, it is one of the sharks' tendencies to question the weak spots of the contestant's proposal. Emotions are definitely not out of the picture because these entrepreneurs probably spent a good length of time to come up with their business plans. Like in any situation when there is a threat of defeat, Shark Tank and Dragon's Den also showcase the desperation and pain of the unsuccessful contestants.

And as the investors probe on the proposal, they have the right to question every aspect of it. The contestant has to be mentally prepared to back his or her proposal. Luckily, when the investors like the business idea, they will state an offer for it. On the other hand, the contestant can also raise a counteroffer if he/she feels that the dragon's offer is too low for his/her idea. However, even if a contestant secures funding on the show, there is still a possibility that it will not push through. Later on the dragons will further test the idea, resources and other relevant details. If this testing period proves that the business plan is still not good enough, the dragons can refuse to continue the funding.

The adapted version of Dragon's Den airs in the United States as ABC's Shark Tank. Its pilot show was aired in January 2009. By September 2013, the show started its 5th season. Six investors better known as the *sharks* include Kevin O'Leary, Barbara Corcoran, Daymond John, Robert Herjavec, Mark Cuban and Lori Greiner.

Moreover, the Dragon's Den adapted version in Canada airs under the same name. The show debuted in 2006 and will be opening its 8th season by October 2013. Dragon's Den is Canada's highest rated reality business show. Current dragons that go with O'Leary are Jim Treliving, Arlene Dickinson, Bruce Croxon, and David Chilton.

CONCLUSION

Thanks again for reading this book!

I hope the information presented in this book has helped you gain insights and ideas on how to set up your business. Setting up your own business is not easy. It is absolutely challenging and daunting but it is well worth the effort.

Being an entrepreneur is not an easy role to fulfill. Moreover, not everyone has what it takes. With the right attitude and the right information, you have better chances of business success. I hope this book has been helpful in this regard.

There are a lot of things and tasks you have to complete and it is best you get started as soon as possible. Do not be afraid to put yourself out there. When you believe in your idea, it may just be worth sharing and well worth pursuing. Put it to test.

Leave your comfort zone and start making things happen. Create value and make a difference in the market. Stomp your mark. With the right attitude and hard work, you should be able to get there. It may take some time before you have an actual taste of success but believe that you will get there eventually!

I hope you have learned something from this book. Let it guide you in your own personal business ventures. Hold nothing back, go out there and find your own success story!

Thank you,

Adrian J. Williams

PS. If you enjoyed this book, please help me out by kindly leaving a review!